D1442736

Smithsonian

LITTLE EXPLORER

CORAL REEFS

by Megan Cooley Peterson

CAPSTONE PRESS
a capstone imprint

Smithsonian Little Explorer is published by Capstone Press, 1710 Roe Crest Drive, North Mankato, Minnesota 56003 www.capstonepub.com

Library of Congress Cataloging-in-Publication Data
Coral reefs / by Megan Cooley Peterson.
pages cm — (Smithsonian little explorer)
Audience: Grades K to 3. Includes index.
Summary: "Introduces coral reefs to young readers, including structure, life cycle, habitat, and other animals and plants that live there"— Provided by publisher.
ISBN 978-1-4765-0247-2 (library binding)
ISBN 978-1-4765-3541-8 (paper over board)
ISBN 978-1-4765-3547-0 (paperback)
ISBN 978-1-4765-3553-1 (ebook PDF)
1. Coral reef biology—Juvenile literature. 2. Coral reefs and islands—Juvenile literature. I. Title.
QH95.8.P48 2014
 578.77′89—dc23   2012050587

Editorial Credits
Kristen Mohn, editor; Sarah Bennett, designer; Marcie Spence, media researcher; Kathy McColley, production specialist

Our very special thanks to Nancy Knowlton, Sant Chair of Marine Sciences, National Museum of Natural History, for her curatorial review. Capstone would also like to thank Kealy Wilson, Smithsonian Institution Project Coordinator and Product Development Manager, and the following at Smithsonian Enterprises: Ellen Nanney, Licensing Manager; Brigid Ferraro, Director of Licensing; Carol LeBlanc, Senior Vice President, Consumer & Education Products.

Image Credits
Alamy Images: Amar and Isabelle Guillen-Guillen Photography, 23 (bottom), Andrew Seale, 23 (middle), Chad Ehlers, 18 (top), ImageState, 16-17, louise murray, 16 (bottom), Michael Patrick O'Neill, 11 (bottom), Reinhard Dirscherl, 26 (top), Richard Whitcombe, 20 (bottom), Stephen Frick Collection, 11 (top), 13; Capstone: 7 (bottom), 18 (bottom); Defenders of Wildlife, 14; Getty Images: David Doubilet/*National Geographic*, 12; Shutterstock: Adrey Armyagov, 9 (bottom), Alvin Yang, 5 (bottom left), Anna Segeren, 6 (top), bluehand, 6 (bottom), Borisoff, 4-5, Brian Kinney, cover, Cattalina, design element, Cigdem Sean Cooper, 24, Dan Exton, 9 (top), James A Dawson, 27, Johan1900, 25 (bottom left), Johan Glindre, 26 (bottom), John A. Anderson, 28, JR Trice, design element, Kim Briers, 2-3, 25 (top), Kristina Vackova, 32, laschi, design element, 5 (bottom right), littlesam, 23 (top right), Manamana, 29, Ocean Image Photography, 22, Orfeev, design element, Paul Duane, 15, Pete Niesen, 17 (bottom right), Peter Leahy, 7 (top), 8, Potapov Alexander, design element, R McIntyre, 19, Ralph Loesche, 5 (top), Rich Carey, 1, 20 (top), Robert Adrian, design element, Shane Gross, 21 (left), Stephen Gibson, 17 (bottom left), stephan kerkhofs, 10, tae208, 23 (top left), Tyler Fox, 30-31, Vilainecrevette, 21 (right), Vlad61, 25 (bottom right)

Printed in the United States of America in Brainerd, Minnesota.
032013   007721BANGF13

TABLE OF CONTENTS

A CITY UNDER THE SEA

A coral reef is like a colorful city under the sea. Plants and animals work together in this underwater ecosystem.

Let's dive into life on a coral reef!

The Great Barrier Reef in Australia can be seen from space!

Hundreds of thousands of kinds of plants and animals live on coral reefs.

sea slug

flamingo tongue snail

WHAT IS A CORAL?

Corals look like plants.
But they are really animals
made up of tiny coral polyps.

coral polyp

Corals are related
to jellyfish.

Coral polyps divide to make more polyps, forming colonies.

HARD CORAL POLYP

TENTACLE
Coral polyps sting plankton and other tiny animals with their tentacles. Then they eat them.

MOUTH
Food enters through the mouth. The mouth is also where waste leaves the coral.

STOMACH

REEF BUILDERS

More than 700 kinds of hard corals help build coral reefs.

Hard coral polyps make limestone skeletons.

These skeletons make up most of a reef.

Living corals grow on top of the skeletons.

Thousands of kinds of plants and animals live on coral reefs.

Soft corals are different from hard corals. Soft corals look like colorful plants swaying in the water. They don't make limestone skeletons.

Coral reefs may grow for thousands of years!

9

ALGAE

Algae help build coral reefs. These plants help glue the reef together.

Some algae live inside hard corals. They help feed corals.

The algae that live in hard corals need lots of sunlight. They turn energy from the sun into food for the corals.

When water temperatures rise, hard corals can lose their helper algae.

Algae give hard corals their color. Without algae, corals lose their color. Some corals may die.

HOW CORAL REEFS FORM

Strong ocean storms can break off pieces of a coral colony. These pieces are carried away.

Coral larvae float through the ocean. They attach to something hard and begin to grow.

They may grow in new places.

New coral reefs also form in other ways.

Large corals grow very slowly. Most only grow about 0.8 inch (2 centimeters) in a year.

WHERE CORAL REEFS GROW

Most coral reefs grow in warm, shallow, ocean water.

Some reefs grow along the shore. Others grow away from land.

Corals need warm temperatures to grow.

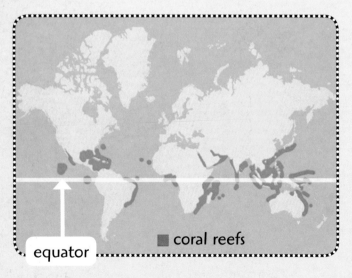

equator

■ coral reefs

Coral reefs are found all around the world near the equator.

KINDS OF CORAL REEFS

Coral reefs are named for where they grow.

FRINGING REEFS

A fringing reef grows close to the shore.
It is usually the smallest kind of reef.

fringing reef

BARRIER REEFS

A barrier reef grows away from the shore. A lagoon sits between a barrier reef and the shore.

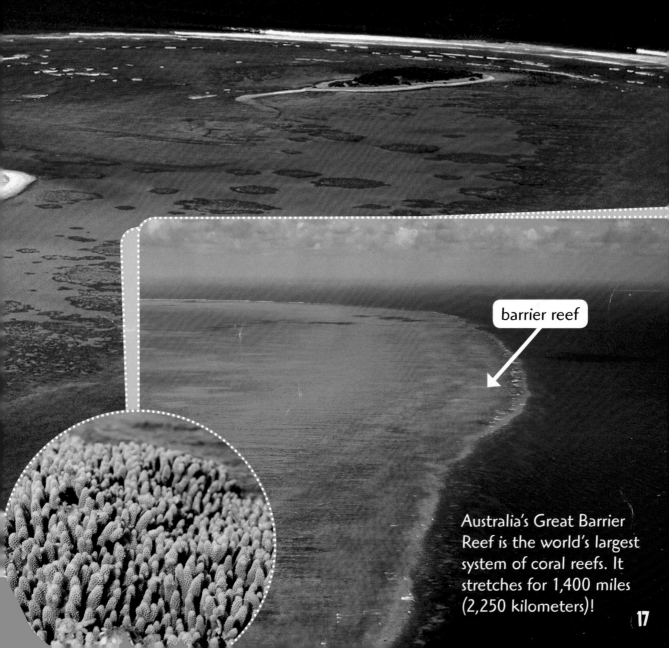

barrier reef

Australia's Great Barrier Reef is the world's largest system of coral reefs. It stretches for 1,400 miles (2,250 kilometers)!

ATOLLS

An atoll is a coral reef in the shape of a ring.

A lagoon sits in the middle of an atoll.

1. fringing reef

2. barrier reef

3. atoll

HOW ATOLLS FORM

1. Most atolls begin as a fringing reef wrapped around an island.

2. The island slowly sinks under the ocean's surface. The fringing reef becomes a barrier reef.

3. The barrier reef becomes an atoll once the island disappears underwater. A lagoon forms in place of the island.

New islands sometimes form on top of atolls.

PLANTS AND CORAL REEFS

Mangrove trees and sea grass beds grow near coral reefs. These plants help clean the water near reefs. They also give reef animals places to hide.

Mangrove tree roots hold down mud and keep it from choking the corals.

Many reef fish hatch in mangrove roots and sea grass beds. The young fish stay safely hidden while they grow.

CORAL REEF FEEDERS

Many ocean creatures find food and homes in a coral reef. They eat the corals, algae, and other animals that grow on the reef.

yellow tube sponge

Many kinds of sponges live on coral reefs. The yellow tube sponge pumps water through the walls of its body. This animal cleans the water by eating bacteria and tiny bits of floating food.

Sea slugs have a ribbon of teeth on their undersides. As they crawl along the reef, the teeth scrape off food.

Crown-of-thorns starfish eat coral polyps. Too many of these starfish on one reef can kill the reef.

The longnose filefish plucks off coral polyps with its pointed mouth.

The blue parrotfish's sharp beak scrapes algae from the reef.

CORAL REEF HUNTERS

Chomp! Coral reef hunters eat animals
that feed on the reef.

Stonefish have lumpy bodies that look like stones. They blend in
with the reef. When fish swim by, the stonefish gobble them up.

Moray eels hide in reef cracks and wait for fish.
The fish don't spot them until it's too late!

Hawksbill sea turtles eat
coral reef sponges.

Cuttlefish are related
to squid and octopuses.
Cuttlefish change colors
to match the reef. They
hide from prey.

Gray reef sharks often swim near coral reefs.
They hunt the hunters! They eat fish, squid, shrimp, and lobsters.

WORKING TOGETHER

Some animals work together on a coral reef. They keep each other safe and clean. They might even share a home!

Shrimp and goby fish live together on the reef. The shrimp digs a burrow. The goby guards their shared home.

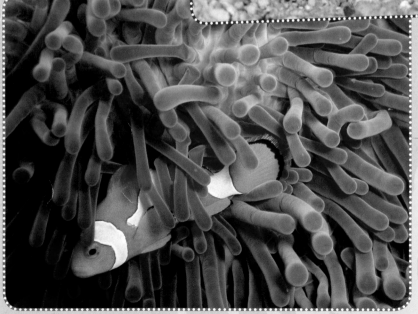

Clown fish live in animals called sea anemones. Clown fish fight other fish that try to eat the anemone. The anemones' tentacles sting the predators. Special slime covers a clown fish's body and protects it from anemone stings.

Cleaner wrasse fish eat parasites off the bodies of fish. Cleaner wrasses even remove unwanted guests from fishes' mouths!

WHY WE NEED CORAL REEFS

Coral reefs provide food and homes for many ocean animals.

Reef animals feed millions of people.

Coral reefs keep people and coasts safe by slowing down strong ocean waves.

About half of the world's coral reefs are under threat. The National Oceanic and Atmospheric Administration (NOAA) works to save coral reefs.

You can help save coral reefs. If you visit a coral reef, do not touch it. Take photos instead.

Scientists find new kinds of coral reef plants and animals every day. They still have much to learn about these important underwater ecosystems.

GLOSSARY

algae—small plants without roots or stems that grow in water

bacteria—very small living things that exist everywhere in nature

burrow—a tunnel or hole in the ground made or used by an animal

ecosystem—a group of animals and plants that live together with their surroundings

equator—an imaginary line around the middle of Earth; it divides the northern and southern hemispheres

lagoon—a body of water between the shore and a reef

larva—a coral polyp at the stage of development between an egg and an adult; more than one larva is called larvae

limestone—a hard rock formed from the skeletons of coral polyps

parasite—an animal or plant that lives on or inside another animal or plant and hurts it

plankton—tiny plants and animals that drift in the sea

polyp—a small sea animal with a tubular body and a round mouth surrounded by tentacles

predator—an animal that hunts other animals for food

prey—an animal hunted by another animal for food

shore—the place where the ocean meets land

CRITICAL THINKING USING THE COMMON CORE

Give an example of how animals work together in the coral reef. (Key Ideas and Details)

The author describes fringing reefs on page 16. What does the word *fringe* mean? What clues in the text help you figure out the meaning? (Craft and Structure)

Look at the map on page 14. Where do coral reefs grow? Why is that a good location for coral reefs? (Integration of Knowledge and Ideas)

READ MORE

Pfeffer, Wendy. *Life in a Coral Reef.* Let's Read and Find Out Science. New York: Collins, 2009.

Rustad, Martha E. H. *Clown Fish and Sea Anemones Work Together.* Animals Working Together. Mankato, Minn.: Capstone Press, 2011.

Salas, Laura Purdie. *Coral Reefs: Colorful Underwater Habitats.* Amazing Science: Ecosystems. Minneapolis: Picture Window Books, 2009.

INTERNET SITES

FactHound offers a safe, fun way to find Internet sites related to this book. All of the sites on FactHound have been researched by our staff.

Here's all you do:

Visit *www.facthound.com*

Type in this code: 9781476502472

Check out projects, games and lots more at
www.capstonekids.com

INDEX